Exploring the Frontiers of Data Encryption

Table of Contents

Chapter 1. Introduction

In our increasingly digital society, the secure transmission and storage of data has never been more critical. This Special Report, "Exploring the Frontiers of Data Encryption," dives headfirst into this vital subject, demystifying the complex world of data encryption for even the least technical readers. Through real-world applications and layman-friendly explanations, the report examines the vanguard of progressive encryption techniques. Whether you're a business manager protecting client information, a student curious about digital privacy, or anyone concerned about the safety of your data in the vast cyberspace, this comprehensive and accessible guide can help equip you with the knowledge you demand. Discover the exciting and rapid evolution of data encryption technology and arm yourself with knowledge in a world where information is the most valuable commodity.

Chapter 2. Understanding the Basics of Data Encryption

The digital age has transformed the way we produce, distribute, and consume information, making the secure management of this data an absolute prerequisite in all industries and facets of life.

2.1. Breaking Down Data Encryption

Data encryption is a process by which information is converted into a code that conceals the original meaning—a protocol as old as communication itself. From the military to business to individual users, communities worldwide have been seeking ways to secure their communication and prevent unauthorized access.

In the digital context, encryption uses an algorithm, also called a cipher, to transmute plaintext information—such as a simple email or a more complex dataset—into ciphertext. This ciphertext appears as an incomprehensible string of random characters to anyone lacking the corresponding decryption key, rendering the original information inaccessible.

2.2. Cipher: The Heart of Encryption

A cipher is a method of encryption and decryption. It can be an algorithm (a sequence of well-defined steps) that transforms plaintext into ciphertext. Historically, ciphers were physical devices, like the Caesar cipher disc or the Enigma machine used during the Second World War. Today, ciphers are computer programs or algorithms used in conjunction with encryption keys. These keys, usually long strings of random letters and numbers, work with the cipher to create the encrypted message.

There are two primary types of encryption ciphers:

- Symmetric-key encryption
- Asymmetric-key encryption

2.3. The Symmetric Key

Symmetric-key encryption, the oldest and most common type, uses the same key for both encryption and decryption. The Caesar Cipher is a type of symmetric encryption where each character in the plaintext is 'shifted' a certain number of places down the alphabet. For example, with a shift of 1, 'A' would be encrypted as 'B' and 'B' would become 'C', and so on.

This type of encryption is fast but has a significant drawback: the key must be securely shared between the sender and the recipient, making it vulnerable to interception.

2.4. Asymmetry in Encryption

Asymmetric-key encryption, also known as public-key encryption, tackles the problem of key sharing. It uses two different but mathematically linked keys: one private and one public. The public key is freely distributed and used to encrypt the message, while the private key, kept secret, is used to decrypt it.

The RSA (Rivest–Shamir–Adleman) algorithm is a well-known example of asymmetric encryption. It is based on the fact that factoring large numbers is computationally intensive and time-consuming, making the encryption secure.

2.5. Encryption Protocols

Encryption protocols, sometimes called cryptographic protocols, are a series of operations that ensure secure communication. Examples of encryption protocols include Secure Sockets Layer (SSL), Transport Layer Security (TLS), Secure Shell (SSH), and Internet Protocol Security (IPSec). They provide a foundation of safety when transmitting data over the Internet.

2.6. Cybersecurity and Data Encryption

Encryption is a significant part of a company's cybersecurity strategy. It protects data at rest (stored data) and data in transit (data sent over networks), safeguarding sensitive information from attackers aiming to steal or manipulate it.

For instance, emails are notoriously vulnerable during transit. Encrypting the contents of an email transforms it into unreadable ciphertext until it reaches the designated recipient, who then uses their decryption key to read it.

2.7. The Constant Evolution of Cryptography

With the rise of quantum computing, a new generation of encryption algorithms is emerging—post-quantum cryptography. Quantum computing utilizes quantum bits (qubits) that can be both 0 and 1 simultaneously, due to their superposition property. This capability could eventually break the current encryption algorithms that rely on the difficulty of factoring large numbers. Post-quantum cryptographic algorithms are being developed to handle this looming threat.

In conclusion, understanding the fundamental aspects of data encryption provides a critical base for the broader exploration of this field. The collective effort to secure our increasingly digitized world will continue to push the boundaries of innovation and fuel the ongoing evolution of encryption technologies.

Chapter 3. Historical Overview of Cryptography

Cryptography, or the practice of securing communication from adversaries, traces its roots back millennia. Humans have been experimenting with secret communication for thousands of years, and as our society has technologically advanced, so too has our ability to encrypt and decrypt messages.

3.1. Ancient Ciphers

The earliest known form of cryptography was found in hieroglyphics carved into the walls of tombs in Egypt around 1900 BC. These weren't used for secrecy, but rather to convey importance or holiness by substituting or reordering symbols.

Considerably later, the Greeks made significant contributions to cryptography around 500 BC with the creation of the "Scytale," a tool used by the Spartans to transport secret messages during wartime. The Scytale consisted of a strip of parchment that was wound around a cylindrical rod. The message was written down the length of the rod and only by wrapping the parchment around an identical rod could the recipient decode the message.

Rome also made strides in cryptography with Julius Caesar's invention of what is known today as the Caesar Cipher, around 58 BC. This cipher is an example of substitution encryption, wherein each letter in the plaintext is substituted with a letter at a fixed number of positions down the alphabet.

3.2. Introduction of Arabic Mathematics

Arabic scholars played an enormous role in advancing cryptography during the middle ages through their major contributions to mathematics, including the development of algebra and algorithms. The philosopher, Al-Kindi, wrote a book in the 9th century on decrypting encrypted code using frequency analysis. This was one of the first instances of recognizable cryptanalysis in history.

3.3. Renaissance Ciphers

The Italian Renaissance was a period of significant advancement in the art of cryptography. During this time, Leon Battista Alberti, an architect by profession, was also actively involved in cipher development. Alberti invented cipher disks, devices for implementing polyalphabetic ciphers, which use multiple substitution alphabets to make frequency analysis significantly more difficult.

In the 16th and 17th centuries, cryptography became essential in diplomacy and warfare. European states started to create permanent offices dealing with cryptography, each with its cipher secretary who was responsible for the encryption and decryption of messages.

3.4. The Industrial Age

In the 19th century, Charles Babbage, an English polymath, made significant contributions to cryptography by breaking the Vigenère cipher, a development of the earlier polyalphabetic principles. His efforts were kept secret at that time due to military secrecy constraints.

The late 19th and 20th centuries witnessed cryptography's significant transition from a mostly manual system to a technologically driven field. The development of mechanical and electromechanical cipher machines marked this change. The Enigma Machine, used by Germany during World War II, is the most well-known of these devices.

3.5. Birth of Modern Cryptography

In the 20th century, with the advent of the digital age, there was a revolutionary change in cryptography, pushing it into the era of modern-day encryption. Data encryption was increasingly based on rigorous mathematical theory, and profound advances in computer technology meant that ciphers could be more complex than ever.

During World War II, both the Allies and the Axis powers used machine-generated ciphers for secrecy. The use of these machines, such as the Enigma machine by the Germans and the American SIGABA, marked a paradigm shift in cryptography from traditional manual methods to more sophisticated and complex mechanical and electromechanical systems.

In the 1970s, symmetric-key algorithms like the Data Encryption Standard (DES) and later Advanced Encryption Standard (AES) became standard for securing electronic data, marking a new era of widespread commercial and governmental use of encryption.

3.6. The Advent of Public-Key Cryptography

In 1976, Whitfield Diffie and Martin Hellman introduced the concept of public-key cryptography. This revolutionary framework allowed secure communication between parties who had no prior knowledge of each other. Utilizing two keys, one public and one private, public-key cryptography enabled secure internet transactions and formed the basis of technologies like SSL and TLS that secure web browsing today.

3.7. Cryptography Today

Cryptographic techniques today are varied and complex, often combining different methods for added security. As technology evolves and grows more sophisticated, so too does the art and science of keeping data secure.

Cryptography is now a foundational aspect of our modern digital world, securing everything from simple text messages to complex banking transactions and classified government information. It has grown far beyond simple character swapping and now includes complex mathematics, computer science, and principles of engineering.

This brief overview barely scratches the surface of cryptography's fascinating and rich history. The complexity and sophistication of modern encryption techniques is vast, as cryptographic scientists continually strive to stay one step ahead of those who would seek to undermine these systems. With each passing day, new techniques are developed, and old ones improved, fueling a never-ending cycle of cryptographic progression. As we continue on into the digital age, the role of cryptography will only become more critical in securing our data and protecting our privacy.

Chapter 4. Types of Encryption: Symmetric and Asymmetric

Today, encryption remains the most effective way to achieve data security. Broadly, it can be split into two categories: symmetric encryption, also known as private key encryption, and asymmetric encryption, also known as public key encryption. Through the course of this section, you will delve into the details of these two major categories, looking at their structure, operation, popular algorithms, advantages, disadvantages, and real-world examples.

4.1. Symmetric Encryption

Symmetric encryption is the oldest and most straightforward type of data encryption. In essence, the process involves one key (a password or algorithm) that is applied to both encrypt and decrypt data. This method is often compared to a simple lock and key mechanism—you apply the key (a password or algorithm) to lock (encrypt) the data, and you use the exact same key to unlock (decrypt) it.

4.1.1. Structure and Operation

In symmetric encryption, both the sender and receiver of data use the same key to encrypt and decrypt the information. As a result, the primary challenge is securely sharing the key with the intended party without it falling into the wrong hands. When the data is about to be sent, the sender applies the key to transform the plaintext (the readable form of the data) into ciphertext (the scrambled form of the data). Upon receiving the data, the receiver applies the same key to the ciphertext, converting it back to plaintext.

4.1.2. Popular Algorithms

Symmetric encryption utilizes several popular algorithms, each with their unique attributes. Here are a few:

1. **Advanced Encryption Standard (AES)**: This algorithm is currently the most popular and widely used symmetric encryption algorithm. It can provide 128-bit, 192-bit, or 256-bit keys and is used across many industries, including in the government sector for encrypting sensitive data.

2. **Data Encryption Standard (DES)**: This was one of the first widely adopted symmetric encryption algorithms, but due to its shorter key length of 56 bit, it was found to be insecure against brute-force attacks. It has largely been replaced by AES.

3. **Triple DES (3DES)**: This is an extension of DES which applies the DES algorithm thrice to each data block. It offers a more secure alternative to its predecessor with a lengthier, 168-bit key, but it is also slower.

4. **Blowfish & Twofish**: These are both symmetric block cipher algorithms. Blowfish has a variable key length up to 448 bits. Twofish is its successor, maintaining similar characteristics but offering protection against more attacks.

4.1.3. Advantages and Disadvantages

Symmetric encryption is highly efficient, making it ideal for encrypting large volumes of data, like database encryption where speed is important. It is faster and less computationally intensive than asymmetric encryption. However, its main disadvantage is the risk surrounding key sharing. Both sender and receiver must have the same key, a situation that may render the key vulnerable to interception.

4.2. Asymmetric Encryption

Asymmetric encryption, sometimes called public key cryptography, uses two related keys, one for encryption and another for decryption. It's a bit more complex than symmetric encryption but offers significant advantages in terms of security, particularly in the realm of digital communication.

4.2.1. Structure and Operation

In asymmetric encryption, each user has a pair of cryptographic keys—a public encryption key and a private decryption key. The public key, as the name suggests, is made available to everyone and is used to encrypt data. In contrast, the private key is kept secret by the key owner and used to decrypt data. The fascinating part is that the two keys are mathematically related in such a way that only the private key can decrypt data encrypted with the public key.

4.2.2. Popular Algorithms

A few of the popular algorithms include:

1. **Rivest-Shamir-Adleman (RSA)**: This is the first algorithm known to be suitable for encryption and digital signatures, as well as key exchange for secure communication.

2. **Diffie-Hellman (DH)**: It is most often used for secure key exchange. In this case, it helps to solve the problem of key distribution and management.

3. **Elliptic Curve Cryptography (ECC)**: ECC generates keys through the properties of the elliptic curve equation instead of the traditional method of generation as the product of very large prime numbers. This approach provides a significantly faster solution with smaller keys and is gaining popularity in industry applications.

4. **ElGamal**: Designed by Taher Elgamal, it is a secure key exchange protocol, widely adopted in PGP (Pretty Good Privacy) and GPG (GNU Privacy Guard) protocols.

4.2.3. Advantages and Disadvantages

Asymmetric encryption offers a stronger security setup as it doesn't require the sharing of decryption keys (private keys) across the network, thus removing the risk prevalent in symmetric encryption. However, it's more resource-intensive than symmetric encryption, meaning it requires more processing power and time. As such, in real-world applications, asymmetric encryption often gets used for securely sharing the encryption keys (used in symmetric encryption) rather than for the encryption of the whole dataset.

In conclusion, both types of encryption play crucial roles in maintaining data integrity and confidentiality in our increasingly digital society. Symmetric encryption, with its relative simplicity and computational efficiency, is ideal for bulk data transmission, while asymmetric encryption, with its improved security measures, excels in securely sharing encryption keys and authenticating identities over public channels. Understanding these systems isn't just beneficial—it's imperative for navigating and safeguarding your digital environment.

Chapter 5. Public Key Infrastructure: A Deep Dive

Even though our lives have become intertwined with the digital world, many people hardly realize how much they depend on a robust and secure system in place to protect their data and privacy. One of such systems is the Public Key Infrastructure (PKI). By supporting the distribution and identification of public encryption keys, the PKI is quintessential to securing communications in networks.

5.1. Understanding Public Key Infrastructure

The foundational structure of PKI rests on two types of cryptographic encryption keys: private and public. Users possess a private key that remains confidential while a public key can be distributed broadly. Messages encrypted with a public key can be decrypted with its connected private key and vice-versa. It's this interchange that allows two parties to secure a line of communication without prior knowledge of each other.

Imagine Alice and Bob, two strangers who wish to share confidential information with each other. Here's how PKI operates:

1. Alice uses Bob's public key to encrypt the message she wants to send.

2. Only Bob, who holds the corresponding private key, can decrypt this message.

3. If Bob wants to prove the message is from him, he can use his private key to encrypt the message.

4. Alice can then decrypt it with Bob's public key, authenticating the

message is indeed from Bob.

Though simplistic, this model is an accurate representation of the concept and offers a glimpse into the power of PKI.

5.2. Infrastructure Components

The five main components of PKI - user, registration authority, certificate authority, directories, and key backup and recovery - are interrelated.

1. The user represents the sender or recipient of the message.
2. Registration authority manages user credentials and initiates the key pair.
3. Certificate authority issues and verifies the digital certificates.
4. Directories store the certificates and certificate revocation lists.
5. Key backup and recovery ensures the safe storage and retrieval of keys.

Together, these components apply an additional security layer by verifying users and managing their cryptographic keys.

5.3. Keys and Digital Certificates

In addition to the above components, PKI makes use of digital certificates. A digital certificate is an electronic credential that verifies the identity of a website or individual. It contains the public key of the certificate holder, their identity information, and the digital signature of the certificate-issuing authority, certifying the authenticity of the public key.

5.4. Ensuring Trust with Certificate Authority (CA)

One of the key players in a PKI is the Certificate Authority (CA). This trusted third party is responsible for issuing and revoking digital certificates. Through the CA, PKI can confirm that a public key attached to a message indeed belongs to the person associated with it. The CA's role is vital for integrity and trust within the sphere of digital communication.

5.5. Security Measures and Constraints

PKI is not without its challenges. For it to perform optimally, security measures like digital certificate lifecycle management, the use of secure key storage and adequately trained personnel are invaluable. With its complex ecosystem, PKI also faces constraints such as operation cost, speed of implementation, and need for regular updates.

5.6. PKI in Real World Applications

PKI finds its usefulness in various online interactions. From secure email transactions to protecting IoT devices; from authenticating financial transactions to buffering the security of eHealth services, PKI has proven indispensable time and again.

In conclusion, with an increasing demand for secure communication, it's hardly surprising that PKI is here not just to stay but to grow. By nurturing an understanding of its operations, we move closer to achieving secure, private digital communications in this broad and expanding cyberspace.

Chapter 6. Salient Features and Limitations of Current Encryption Techniques

Data encryption's utility is underpinned by its ability to convert readable data, or plaintext, into unreadable cipher, or ciphertext, allowing information to be securely transmitted in seemingly up-for-grabs digital environments. Today, various encryption techniques, each harboring unique features and occasional limitations, are employed for this purpose. This chapter will delve into exploring these salient attributes.

6.1. Symmetric Encryption: Building a Shared Cryptographic Key

Symmetric encryption is among the most common techniques used today. This method involves one key that is employed for both the encryption and decryption of data, a paragon of strength and simplicity that is not without fault.

To begin with, symmetric encryption offers speed. Since the same key is used to lock and unlock the data, the processing requirements are minimized, allowing for rapid information encryption and decryption. This pace makes symmetric encryption ideally suited for securing high volumes of data or real-time data transmission, as seen with streaming services and sensitive databases.

Next, symmetric encryption is renowned for its robust security. Techniques such as the Advanced Encryption Standard (AES) no longer compute merely 64-bit but go up to 256-bit encryption. This creates an astronomically large number of potential decryption keys, providing formidable resistance against brute force attacks.

However, symmetric encryption is plagued with key distribution problems, since the same key is kept on all user systems. Securely distributing this key without it being intercepted represents one of the most significant challenges with symmetric encryption. While secure communication channels can minimize this risk, they are rarely practical for broad-scale deployment.

6.2. Asymmetric Encryption: Pairing Private and Public Keys

Asymmetric encryption, or public-key cryptography, addresses the limitations of symmetric encryption by employing a pair of keys: one public, and another private. The public key is available to anyone, while the private one is kept secret. The data encrypted with the public key can only be decrypted with the paired private key, and vice versa.

The foremost advantage of an asymmetric system is its ability to disseminate public keys openly without the associated security concerns. This promotes easy and efficient key distribution as there's no need to privately share a single symmetric key.

Another advantage is heightened security. Since the private key never leaves the user's possession, it reduces the risk of key compromise. This robust security makes it suitable for securing sensitive transactions, such as those found in e-commerce and banking.

However, asymmetric encryption's increased complexity results in increased computational requirements and subsequently slower processing times. This makes it less suited for large-scale, real-time data transmissions. Furthermore, the security of asymmetric encryption is only as good as the security of the private key, needing strong measures in place to protect it from being compromised.

6.3. Hybrid Encryption: The Best of Both Worlds

Hybrid encryption techniques combine symmetric and asymmetric encryption to harness the benefits of both. In this approach, symmetric encryption is used for data transmission due to its speed, while asymmetric encryption secures the symmetric key due to its superior key distribution capabilities.

This amalgamation of methods ensures high-speed, high-security data circulation while overcoming the key distribution problems associated with symmetric encryption. However, it also inherits the relative slowness from asymmetric encryption and the need for robust private key protection.

6.4. Hash Functions: Guaranteeing Data Integrity

Hash functions play a vital role in data verification, creating a unique 'signature' for a given data input. They enhance data integrity and authentication, ensuring a file's authenticity by checking that its hash value matches the initial value after transmission.

While not an encryption method per se, hash functions are integral to verification. They are extremely fast and yield unique hashes for each unique input. However, they possess a one-way functionality; data processed into a hash cannot be reversed to regain the original data.

The science and art of data encryption are fast-evolving, pressing against its own limitations while giving birth to novel methodologies. This constant innovation is tasked with the heavy responsibility of keeping our vast seas of data safe from prying eyes. Although the techniques outlined in this chapter represent the vanguard of encryption technology, they are merely the tip of the iceberg in the dynamic and exciting world of data encryption.

Chapter 7. Anatomy of End-to-End Encryption

As the internet continues to permeate every sphere of life, it becomes essential to know its particular language and technicalities. One language you'll often hear spoken in cybersecurity circles is that of end-to-end encryption.

End-to-end encryption is a method of secure data transmission that prevents third parties, including internet providers, telecommunications operators, and even the service provider itself, from accessing data while it's transferred between devices.

To understand how end-to-end encryption functions, let's break it down to its primary components and processes.

7.1. The Concept of End-to-End Encryption

End-to-end encryption is based on principles of cryptography. Cryptography is the study of secure communication techniques, which allow only the intended parties to read the information. It involves transforming plaintext information into a format that can't be understood (cipher), and changing it back into its original form. With end-to-end encryption, this process occurs at the two "ends" of a communication: input (encryption) and output (decryption).

This encryption method has been widely adopted due to its effectiveness in protecting the privacy and security of data exchange over the internet. It's a crucial aspect of systems that deal with sensitive information, such as banking apps, messaging platforms, and email services.

7.2. Keys and Their Role in Encryption

The process of encryption and decryption revolves around 'keys.' In a physical environment, if you have a box which you want to lock, you will use a physical key. Similarly, in the digital world, we use virtual or digital 'keys' to lock (encrypt) and unlock (decrypt) data.

A key is a random string of bits created explicitly for scrambling and unscrambling data. We have two types of keys used in end-to-end encryption - the Public Key and the Private Key, collectively called Key Pairs.

- The Public Key: This encryption key is made public, meaning anyone can use it to encrypt a message. However, once the message is encrypted with a public key, it can only be decrypted with the paired private key.

- The Private Key: This decryption key remains strictly confidential to the owner. It is used to decrypt the data that has been encrypted by its paired public key.

7.3. Public Key Infrastructure (PKI) and Certificate Authorities

End-to-End encryption makes use of Public Key Infrastructure (PKI), a system that issues digital certificates to assert the validity of public keys. In essence, PKI is designed to create a trustworthy environment for the exchange of information over unsecure networks, such as the Internet.

PKI is governed by Certificate Authorities (CA). These trusted entities verify the identities of the parties involved and issue digital certificates. A certificate contains information about the owner's identity, their public key, the certificate's validity period, and the digital signature of the CA that confirms the certificate has been issued by a trusted source.

7.4. How End-to-End Encryption Works

In practice, the process of end-to-end encryption begins when a user sends data:

1. The sender's system uses the recipient's public key to encrypt the message.

2. This encrypted message is then sent over the internet, safe from uninvited onlookers because it can only be decrypted using the recipient's private key.

3. Once the message reaches the recipient, their system uses their private key to decrypt the message, turning it back into its original, understandable form.

4. To reply, the recipient now becomes the sender, and their system uses the original sender's public key to encrypt the response. The process is then repeated.

This cycle ensures that only the authorized parties—those with the correct private keys—can access the original, decrypted data.

7.5. The Importance of Secure Key Exchange

Since the security of end-to-end encryption hinges on keeping the private keys confidential, the process of distributing these keys—known as Key Exchange or Key Distribution—is critical.

There are several methods of key exchange that offer different balances between security and practicality. One widely used method is the Diffie-Hellman Key Exchange, which is both secure and efficient. It allows two devices to each generate a public-private key pair and exchange their public keys in a way that an intercepted public key cannot be linked to its associated private key.

7.6. The Role of SSL/TLS in End-to-End Encryption

Secure Sockets Layer (SSL) and its successor, Transport Layer Security (TLS), play a vital role in end-to-end encryption, especially on the Web. These cryptographic protocols provide secure communications over a network by encrypting the data on the sender's device and decrypting it on the recipient's device. This process assures the confidentiality and integrity of data, regardless of the unsecured nature of the network it traverses.

SSL/TLS works by using a combination of Symmetric and Asymmetric encryption. Asymmetric encryption is used in the initial 'Handshake' to securely distribute the keys needed for Symmetric encryption, which is then used for the rest of the communication due to its efficiency.

Overall, mastering the anatomy of end-to-end encryption equips users with a thorough understanding of how their data is kept secure during online exchanges. As the digital world continues to evolve, staying educated about data security technologies is a must for anyone interacting with the web. With a firm grasp on these principles, you're better positioned to make informed decisions regarding your digital privacy and security.

Chapter 8. The Intersection of Blockchain and Encryption

The burgeoning evolution of technology has seen data cease being just mere information, transforming into a priceless asset that needs protection now more than ever. The rampant digitization across all economic sectors has espoused technologies like encryption and blockchain to achieve secure data transmission and storage. Although these technologies function in different spheres, their intersection creates a research-intensive hotspot, explored herein.

8.1. Understanding Blockchain and Encryption

Blockchain and encryption, at first glance, might seem technologically arduous for non-tech enthusiasts. However, knowing their basic operation is the first step towards understanding their integration.

Encryption, dating back to the era of ancient Rome, is a method of scrambling data into a code that hides its actual meaning, thus safeguarding it from unauthorized access. While the encryption process, known as encryption algorithm, is public, the key used to encrypt and decrypt the data is secret, providing the security layer. Encrypting data before transmitting it over the Internet rejuvenates the fight against cybercrime, protecting communication from interception.

Blockchain technology, on the other hand, introduces a decentralized, transparent, and secure data storage platform. A blockchain is a continually growing list of records (blocks) linked using cryptography, a discipline that encompasses encryption. Each block carries data, the hash of the block (a unique identifier), and the hash of the previous block, linking the blocks creating the blockchain. This chain grows with every new data entry, thus forming a digital ledger immune to data modification after entry. Thanks to the transparency and security, its most popular application is in cryptocurrencies, like Bitcoin.

8.2. Convergence of Blockchain and Encryption

The merging of blockchain and encryption propels cybersecurity a notch higher. It helps mitigate data breaches, tampering, theft, and unauthorized access, among other cybercrimes. It does so by employing cryptographic algorithms on blockchain technology, thus enhancing transaction confidentiality and data privacy.

In a blockchain, data is encrypted using a process called cryptographic hashing before adding to any block. Hashing turns data into a unique series of characters irrespective of the data size. Intruders, therefore, cannot reverse-engineer data even if they manage to decipher one hashed output given the hash functions' uniqueness. Furthermore, the hash of each block connects to its previous one; hence suspects can't tamper with data without detection as it would disrupt the entire chain.

8.3. Impact on Data Privacy

Incorporating encryption in blockchain not only strengthens cybersecurity but also bolsters data privacy. Blockchain provides a transparent and secure framework for transmitting information. Adding encryption into the mix promotes the privacy of the data, which is vital in sectors that handle sensitive data, such as the health industry. In such places, patient information, financial data, or personal identifiers require utmost protection against unauthorized access and potential misuse.

8.4. The role of Public Key Infrastructure (PKI)

The importance of Public Key Infrastructure (PKI) at this intersection cannot be understated. PKI is a system of digital certificates, Certificate Authorities, and other registration authorities that verify and authenticate each involved party's validity in data transfer. In blockchain technology, PKI establishes secure cryptography for every transaction, maintaining the integrity and confidentiality of the data.

8.5. Blockchain and Encryption in Cryptocurrency

Arguably, the most popular intersection of blockchain and encryption is in cryptocurrency. It provides secure transaction verification, vital considering the financial implications of secure transactions in digital currency markets. Here, encryption pairs with blockchain to offer secure, transparent, and unalterable transaction records.

8.6. Future Prospects

As innovative minds work tirelessly to enhance data protection, the intersection of blockchain and encryption will remain a research hotspot. Their convergence holds the promise to revolutionize sectors like finance, health, and even government operations by providing secure, transparent, and indestructible data management methods.

In summary, understanding the intricate details of encryption and blockchain's symbiosis is no easy task; however, the benefits far outweigh the challenges. This intersection presents a novel pathway to achieving secure and transparent digital transactions and storage, which is a necessity in this Internet-dominated era. By continually bolstering cybersecurity and data privacy measures, blockchain and encryption can continue to safeguard our digital lives in ever-evolving ways.

Chapter 9. Data Encryption and Cybersecurity Laws

Data encryption plays a crucial role in protecting information—whether it's your bank account details, your company's strategic documents, or your personal emails—from unauthorized individuals. Equally, cybersecurity laws enforced globally ensure that these security techniques are used appropriately and that data breaches are penalized.

9.1. Understanding Data Encryption

Data encryption is the encoding of information into a form that only authorized parties can access. It uses an algorithm to transform readable data, referred to as plaintext, into an unreadable, encrypted format—otherwise known as ciphertext. Only those with a specific key can decode, or decrypt, this information, and make it understandable again.

Two primary types of data encryption exist, symmetric and asymmetric encryption. Symmetric encryption involves a single key for both encrypting and decrypting information. This method is faster and ideal for bulk data. However, the challenge lies in safely transmitting the encryption key. If it falls into the wrong hands, the protected data can be easily compromised.

On the other hand, asymmetric encryption uses a pair of mathematically related keys: a public key for encryption and a private key for decryption. The public key is freely distributed, but the private key is kept secret by the key owner. Since the keys are different for encryption and decryption, it reduces the risk during key transmission. However, this type of encryption is slower due to computational complexity and it's not ideal for large data volumes.

9.2. The Role of Encryption in Cybersecurity

Cybersecurity is an umbrella term encompassing measures adopted to protect data and systems from cyber-attacks. Encryption, being one of these measures, serves multiple purposes. It protects data during transmission between systems and during storage—when data is at rest. Even in case of a data breach, encrypted data remains unreadable and useless without the decryption key.

Encryption also helps maintain data integrity by preventing unauthorized alterations, and confirm data authenticity via digital signatures and certificates.

9.3. Impact of Quantum Computing on Data Encryption

Quantum computing, with its computational leap, poses a substantial threat to current encryption methodologies. Quantum computers exploit the strange ability of subatomic particles to exist in more than one state at any time. Due to the bizarre nature of quantum theories, operations can be done much more quickly and use less energy than classical computers. In the future, quantum computers might crack encryption algorithms that are currently considered secure.

However, the encryption landscape is preparing to meet this challenge head-on. Post-quantum cryptography is an area of growing research interest. These cryptographic methods should be able to withstand attacks from both classical and future quantum computers, ensuring the longevity and security of encrypted data.

9.4. Global Cybersecurity Laws and Regulations

Cybersecurity laws differ greatly from one jurisdiction to the next. However, they all aim to protect personal and business data from cyber threats. Some countries, like the United States, take a sectorial approach, where laws are formulated according to the type of data or the industry sector. This includes laws such as the Health Insurance Portability and Accountability Act (HIPAA) for health data and the Gramm-Leach-Bliley Act (GLBA) for financial records.

In contrast, the European Union's General Data Protection Regulation (GDPR) has a broad scope, aiming to protect all personally identifiable information. Non-compliance with GDPR regulations could result in substantial penalties.

9.5. Encryption Laws Across Different Jurisdictions

Some countries have specific laws related to the use of encryption. For instance, countries like Russia and China have explicit rules demanding to access encrypted data, appropriate backdoor keys from firms, and limit the high-level of anonymized encryption. Still, others like Australia, have enacted laws that can compel tech companies to provide assistance when it comes to accessing encrypted communication.

In the USA, the encryption policy is complex and controversial. The strong encryption helps the economy and supports privacy. However, law enforcement agencies argue that it also aids criminals. Thus, a cipher war between privacy advocates and government agencies continues, with no apparent resolution in sight.

9.6. Encryption Backdoors and Their Controversy

Encryption backdoors are deliberate vulnerabilities put into encryption algorithms or key management processes by design or request to give third-party agents, typically governmental organizations, access to the encrypted data. These backdoors are controversial. While they can help in law enforcement or state surveillance for national security, the very presence of a backdoor also introduces vulnerabilities that could be exploited by ill-intentioned parties.

9.7. The Future of Data Encryption and Cybersecurity Laws

As technology continues to evolve, so will data encryption techniques and cybersecurity laws. Artificial Intelligence and Machine Learning could be employed to automate and enhance cybersecurity measures. Unarguably, we will continue to see an escalation in cyber threats and cybercrime activities alongside these advancements, underscoring the need for persistent vigilance and advancement within the cybersecurity and legal sectors.

Overall, encryption plays an indispensable role in our digital world, protecting our data from being misused or stolen. It is up to us to stay informed about how these technologies are changing and regulated, so we can better protect ourselves and adapt to the successively digital future.

Chapter 10. Future of Data Encryption: Quantum Cryptography and Beyond

The universe of cryptographic systems, as it stands today, is predominantly founded on the computational hardness of certain problems. Cryptographic systems take advantage of problems that are currently unfeasible to solve in a reasonable time frame with the computational resources we have now. One such infamous problem is factoring large integers into primes, the foundation of the widely used RSA encryption protocol. However, with the rapid advancement of computational prowess and the emergence of quantum computers that promise exponential leaps in processing power, many existing encryption methodologies may become vulnerable. This potential future is at the heart of discussions on Quantum Cryptography and Beyond.

10.1. The Advent of Quantum Computing

Quantum computers manipulate 'qubits' instead of traditional binary bits, enabling them to run intricate computations at unfathomable speeds. Theoretically, this quantum advantage enables the factoring of large integers rapidly, introducing cracks in the bedrock of our current encryption infrastructure. While we're still years from realizing practical, large scale quantum computers, the theoretical threat they pose to existing cryptographic systems is already influencing research in cryptography.

A quantum computer's threats to today's encryption algorithms stem from Shor's Algorithm, which instructs quantum computers on factoring large integers efficiently. As an example, a quantum computer equipped with tens of thousands of fault-tolerant qubits could theoretically break today's RSA encryption in less than a second, a task that would take a classical computer several billion years.

However, quantum computers extend beyond threats, they also promise the development of new cryptographic systems that could effectively resist even quantum decryption attacks. This leads us to the new frontier of what is known as Quantum Cryptography.

10.2. Quantum Cryptography: An Overview

Quantum Cryptography leverages the principles of quantum physics to achieve encryption. The most popular method within this domain is Quantum Key Distribution (QKD), which offers a method for two parties to generate a shared secret key. The security of this key is based not on the hardness of computational problems, as with classical methods, but upon the laws of physics.

In QKD, a stream of quantum particles, like light photons, is sent from one party to another. Each particle's state is changed to encode information. If an eavesdropper attempts to intercept this transmission and measure a photon's state, its quantum state would be altered and the intrusion would be discovered — this is a consequence of the Heisenberg Uncertainty Principle. This enables QKD to offer guaranteed, unconditional security.

However, QKD is not a silver bullet solution. It's currently expensive, complex, and challenging to scale, with limitations on transmission distance. Moreover, it addresses only the transmission of keys, not the encryption and decryption operations — where classical cryptographic algorithms are still needed.

10.3. The Post-Quantum Cryptography

With the concerns over Quantum Computing breaking the currently used encryption protocols, and given the hurdles in the broad application of Quantum Cryptography, we now enter the domain of Post-Quantum Cryptography (PQC). PQC refers to cryptographic systems that, although run on classical computers, are designed to remain secure even in the face of quantum attacks.

Because it is not yet apparent which of these will be the most suitable, PQC is currently a fertile area of exploration and possibility, with multiple families of algorithms under consideration. These include lattice-based, code-based, multivariate polynomial, and hash-based systems, each with their unique characteristics, strengths, and weaknesses.

In the lattice-based approach, the security is derived from the Shortest Vector Problem (SVP) and Closest Vector Problem (CVP), which are considered hard to solve, even on quantum machines. Similarly, the hashing algorithms rely on mathematical functions that maintain their level of difficulty with quantum computers.

10.4. The Path Forward

As we hurtle towards the Quantum Age, it's crucial to prepare our encryption infrastructure for the seismic shifts it incurs. This process, known as "quantum-proofing", involves updating cryptographic standards and systems to post-quantum standard to safeguard our digital world.

Standardizing new quantum-resistant encryption algorithms is a massive undertaking. Organizations such as the National Institute of Standards and Technology (NIST) in the United States are leading the way, hoping to finalize a new standard by 2022.

Additionally, it's equally important that we continue to scale quantum cryptographic methods even as we work to bolster classical ones. This dual approach is most likely to lead us to a well-rounded stable of cryptographic tools that will serve us in an age of quantum computing.

In the end, despite the uncertainties and challenges that come with technological advancement, one thing is clear: the future of data encryption is set to be an intricate jumble of classical, quantum, and post-quantum cryptography. It is in the exploration and amalgamation of these approaches that we can find the most sturdy and resilient pathways for safe and secure transmission of data in the future.

Chapter 11. Critical Measures for Enhancing Personal Encryption Security

Secure communications and data storage demand robust encryption measures. They form the backbone in protecting personal data from unauthorized access and potential misuse. As instances of data breaches and cyberattacks skyrocket, it becomes imperative for individuals to understand and implement effective measures to heighten personal encryption security. Let's start this deep dive by examining the core concepts behind encryption.

11.1. Understanding Encryption

Encryption, at its most basic level, involves transforming readable information, referred to as plaintext, into an unreadable format, called ciphertext. An encryption key accomplishes this conversion, making it incomprehensible to anyone without the correct decryption key. There are two primary types of encryption: symmetric, where the same key is used for both encryption and decryption; and asymmetric, where different keys are used – a public key for encryption and a private key for decryption.

11.2. Importance of Strong Encryption Keys

The strength of an encryption strategy significantly depends on its keys. A robust encryption software fails the moment a weak or compromised key is employed. Implementing strong and complex encryption keys is your first line of defense in enhancing your encryption security. Such keys remain highly resistant to brute force attacks, wherein cybercriminals attempt to crack encryption by trying every possible key combination.

11.3. Updating Encryption Algorithms

In the world of data cryptography, evolving and updating encryption algorithms is pivotal. Cryptanalysts and hackers are constantly on the prowl, attempting to break through existing algorithms. Once they decipher how an algorithm functions, it's only a matter of time before they crack the code. Therefore, it's essential to keep your encryption algorithms up-to-date with the latest advancements, ensuring that your data always has the most robust protection.

11.4. Implementing Secure Transmission Practices

To keep data secure during transmission, employing ways such as secure sockets layer (SSL), transport layer security (TLS), or their successor protocol, HTTPS, is paramount. These ensure that data in transit between networks is encrypted, thus securing transactions lined up in the transmission chain, such as login information or credit card transactions.

11.5. Understanding Encryption Software Options

While numerous encryption software options exist, two primary categories reign: disk encryption software and file encryption software. Disk encryption encrypts every bit of data on a disk or disk partition. On the other hand, file encryption software encrypts individual files. Knowledge about these software options can inform your decision on which one best suits your encryption requirements.

11.6. Staying Vigilant Against Phishing Attacks

Phishing attempts often pave the way for encryption breaches. Through deceptive emails or messages, hackers can convince unsuspecting individuals to provide sensitive information or unknowingly download malware. Guarding against phishing requires knowledge about these attacks to recognize them before they can compromise your encryption.

11.7. Regularly Updating Software

Regularly updating all software is a crucial yet often overlooked security practice. Updates not only provide new features and bug fixes but also carry patches for identified security vulnerabilities. Failing to promptly update software can leave your system at the mercy of cybercriminals who exploit these vulnerabilities.

11.8. Utilizing Virtual Private Networks (VPNs)

VPNs serve as an additional layer of security and privacy. By creating a dedicated network connection where all of your data is encrypted and transmitted securely, VPNs make an integral addition to personal encryption security.

11.9. Employing Multi-Factor Authentication

Multi-factor authentication (MFA) provides an additional defense layer. Even if an attacker cracks your encryption, they still need to bypass MFA, which requires the user to provide at least two identification factors: something they know (such as a password), something they have (like a hardware token), or something they are (biometric data).

While the tenets of personal encryption security appear complex, they can be distilled into these critical measures. When employed proactively, they offer robust encryption security, safeguarding personal data from the prying eyes of cybercriminals. Strengthening your knowledge of data encryption and implementing these measures is not just a necessity in this digital age – it's an imperative.